PAINTING CHILDREN
IN WATERCOLOR

PORTRAIT OF A GIRL AND HER DOLL

PAINTING CHILDREN
IN WATERCOLOR

Herb Olsen, A.N.A.

BONANZA BOOKS • NEW YORK

© MCMLX, REINHOLD PUBLISHING CORPORATION

ALL RIGHTS RESERVED

PRINTED IN THE UNITED STATES OF AMERICA

LIBRARY OF CONGRESS CATALOG CARD NO. 60-15925

DESIGNED BY MYRON HALL III

This edition published by Bonanza Books,
a division of Crown Publishers, Inc.,
by arrangement with Reinhold Publishing Corporation.
A B C D E F G

CONTENTS

List of Color Plates   7
Foreword   8

I. DRAWING THE CHILD: BASIC FORMS   11
    Proportion   12
    KAREN   18
    Painting Instructions for KAREN   21

II. THE CHILD IN ACTION   23
    THREE HAITIAN GIRLS IN BLUE   28
    Painting Instructions for THREE HAITIAN GIRLS IN BLUE
       with Step-by-step Illustrations   30
    MOTHER'S HELPER   33
    THE SISTERS   33
    Painting Instructions for MOTHER'S HELPER
       with Step-by-step Illustrations   34
    Afterthought: MOTHER'S HELPER   36
    Painting Instructions for THE SISTERS
       with Step-by-step Illustrations   38
    AT THE BEACH   40
    Painting Instructions for AT THE BEACH
       with Step-by-step Illustrations   42

III. PORTRAITURE   51
    Drawing the Head   52
    Asymmetry of the Face   56
    Hair Styles   57
    Painting the Head: SUSAN   58
    Painting Instructions for SUSAN
       with Step-by-step Illustrations   62
    Expressions   64
    The Portrait in Monochrome Watercolor   66
    The Portrait in Line and Wash   68
    Portraits: Pen and Ink and Lithograph Pencil   70
    PORTRAIT OF A GIRL AND HER DOLL   72
    Painting Instructions for PORTRAIT OF A GIRL AND HER DOLL
       with Step-by-step Illustrations   80

(continued on page 6.)

IV. THE CHILD IN HIS OWN ENVIRONMENT ... 83

THE WAIF ... 84

THE YOUNG FISHERMAN ... 88

Painting Instructions for THE YOUNG FISHERMAN ... 91

THE TIGHTROPE WALKER ... 93

Painting Instructions for THE TIGHTROPE WALKER ... 95

Cropping a Picture ... 96

The Simple Figure ... 98

Acetate ... 100

DEEP WATER ... 103

V. MATERIALS AND HOW TO USE THEM ... 105

The Palette ... 106

Mixing Paint ... 108

CAMARADERIE ... 110

Painting Instructions for CAMARADERIE ... 112

Brushes ... 115

The Fan Brush ... 119

Position of the Paper ... 121

The Sponge ... 122

Maskoid ... 123

VI. PORTFOLIO OF CANDID PHOTOGRAPHS ... 124

COLOR PLATES

PORTRAIT OF A GIRL AND HER DOLL ... frontispiece

KAREN ... 19

THREE HAITIAN GIRLS IN BLUE ... 29

MOTHER'S HELPER ... 32

THE SISTERS ... 32

AT THE BEACH ... 41

SUSAN—A Painting Demonstration ... 60–61

PORTRAIT OF A GIRL AND HER DOLL—A Painting Demonstration ... 80

THE WAIF ... 89

THE YOUNG FISHERMAN ... 89

THE TIGHTROPE WALKER ... 92

DEEP WATER ... 102

CAMARADERIE ... 111

ACKNOWLEDGMENTS

I would like to express my thanks to my wife Doris who collaborated with me in the preparation of this book—for the countless hours she spent in writing the text, and for her patient understanding of the problems involved.

I would also like to thank my friend Dr. Theodore Merolla who took the color photographs and many of the black and whites. His skill and knowledge in the field of photography have contributed greatly to the presentation of the material. His enthusiasm and painstaking work were a constant source of inspiration.

FOREWORD

The growth of interest in watercolor painting in recent years is extremely gratifying to those of us in the profession. Watercolor was once regarded as the most difficult painting medium to master and misconceptions about it were widespread. However, the old aura of fear and trembling has been dispelled—largely due to improved teaching methods and instruction books. Today, more and more people are using their increased leisure time to learn the fascination of watercolor painting.

A particular source of satisfaction to me has been the enthusiastic response to my first book, *Watercolor Made Easy* (1955), and its sequel, *Painting the Figure in Watercolor* (1958). Since the publication of these books, countless people have expressed interest in the special problems of painting children in watercolor. Many were students in my classes who had made progress in painting the figure and wished to go on to paint their own children. Of course, parenthood is not a requisite for a desire to paint children—for their vitality and fresh purity of coloring make them an appealing subject to any painter. Upon investigation I found that there were virtually no books available on painting children in watercolor. Thus, I felt that such an instruction book would fulfill a real need.

This book is not directed to the complete beginner but rather to the painter who has had some experience in watercolor. However, a certain amount of basic material is included because, in my twenty years of teaching experience, I have often found that

I was taking too much knowledge on the part of the student for granted. Here, I have attempted to show how to capture the essence of the child in watercolor in as simplified a way as possible.

The need for a careful preliminary drawing is stressed, as well as the value of using Basic Forms in establishing proportion, and action, and in planning composition. Portraiture and the special problems presented by children as subjects are discussed in detail. The importance of depicting the child in his own environment is explained, with emphasis on the part that backgrounds play in creating moods such as nostalgia, humor, fantasy, and so forth. Many facets of watercolor painting are explained throughout the book, and, in addition, a special section is devoted entirely to materials and their use. A number of candid photographs are also included for reference.

Most of the paintings reproduced in color are accompanied by step-by-step descriptions of how they were painted; these constitute a most important feature of the book. Simplified palettes have been worked out for some of the paintings such as "Susan," and "Three Haitian Girls in Blue;" the less experienced painter would do well to start with these.

Although there is no substitute for personal teaching, I believe that carrying out this type of step-by-step instruction is the next best way of learning how to paint. As in other disciplines, constant practice is essential and will provide its own rewards.

BASIC FORM

PROPORTION WITHIN THE FIGURE

BASIC
SHAPES

BASIC
PLEATS

FIGURE REFINED

I. DRAWING THE CHILD:

BASIC FORMS

My approach to the drawing of any subject—whether a landscape or figure, adult or child—is basically the same. First I look for the large masses, which I call the Basic Forms, and set these down. This clearly shows the structure of the painting and establishes relative proportion in a very simplified way. In planning a composition, this procedure provides the first big breakdown of major areas. In drawing a single figure without a background, it insures the proper placement of the figure on the paper.

In drawing the figure of the child—the problem we are concerned with here—the use of Basic Forms is most helpful in establishing proportion within the figure. It minimizes the danger, for example, of ending up with a drawing of a head that is too small for the body, arms that are too short, and so forth.

After the largest Basic Form of the whole figure has been drawn, the main parts of the body—the head, torso, arms, and legs are drawn as Basic Forms in the same manner and then refined, as illustrated in the drawings on page 10. This procedure can be followed even for the individual features. Drawing the head and features will be discussed in detail in the section on Portraiture.

PROPORTION

Although some knowledge of anatomy is a requisite for drawing a figure skillfully, in a book such as this where we are primarily concerned with painting in watercolor, it is not possible to include a lengthy discussion of anatomy. Many good books devoted exclusively to this subject are available to the student.

In drawing children there are certain general things to keep in mind. First in importance is how to establish the relative proportion of the head to the body. By using the head as a rough unit of measurement a simple "heads high" gauge is established. This is one of the primary devices in measure a figure whether adult or child. The chart shown here gives some idea of the relative proportions of children from one to ten years old. You will see that the younger the child, the larger his head in proportion to his body. Once the proportion of the head to the body is established, the first problem in drawing the figure has been solved.

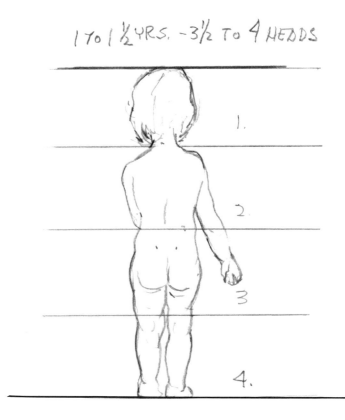

I TO I ½ YRS. -3½ TO 4 HEADS

1.

2.

3.

4.

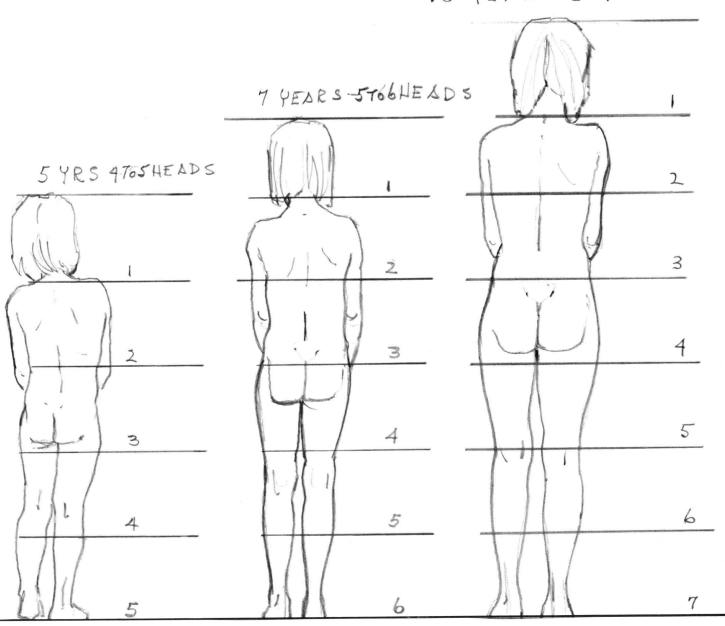

5 YRS 4To5 HEADS

7 YEARS - 5To6 HEADS

10 YEARS - 6To7 HEADS

PROPORTIONS AT VARIOUS AGES
(APPROXIMATE)

13

Look for the Basic Forms.

MAKE SEVERAL
SHAPES.
IT WILL
LOOSEN YOU UP!

A SEAL

NOTE HOW BASIC SHAPE
RESEMBLES A DUCK

DRAW FIGURE
WITH VARIED LINE
IT HELPS GIVE THE
FIGURE FORM

IN MAKING THE BASIC SHAPE
USE A PHOTOGRAPH OR DRAW IT
FROM LIFE. DON'T JUST MAKE A SHAPE

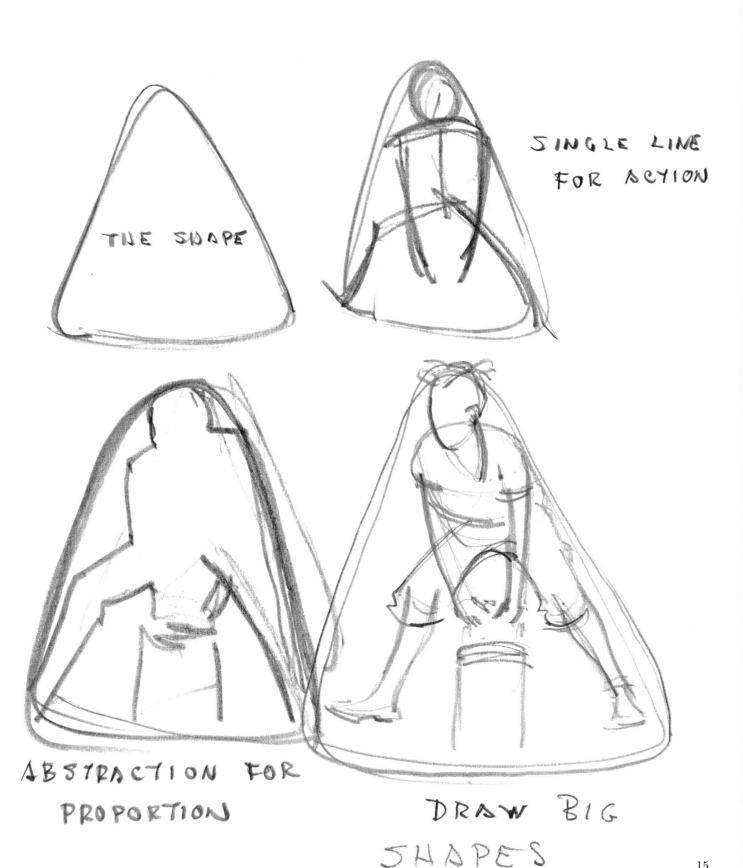

THE SHAPE

SINGLE LINE FOR ACYION

ABSTRACTION FOR PROPORTION

DRAW BIG SHAPES

Use Basic Forms to establish proportion.

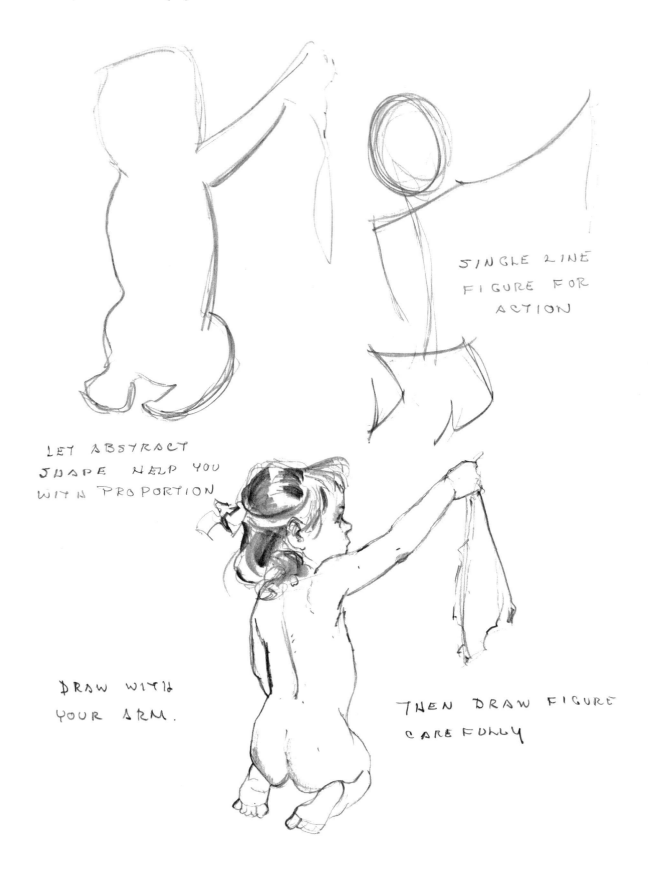

SINGLE LINE
FIGURE FOR
ACTION

LET ABSTRACT
SHAPE HELP YOU
WITH PROPORTION

DRAW WITH
YOUR ARM.

THEN DRAW FIGURE
CAREFULLY

KAREN

Living close to Long Island Sound, I have had many opportunities to observe and study children playing at the beach. I have often been fascinated by their intense efforts in building castles in the sand, and sometimes wished that all this energy could be diverted into a more lasting enterprise, or that a budding architect might develop out of it. While watching such an operation one day, I saw a little girl happily dousing herself with water from a sprinkling can to refresh herself after her efforts. I quickly took a snapshot of her for action and lighting. From this I made a few rough sketches before the preliminary drawing. The subject—about a 5-year-old—held a particular attraction for me, not only because of the interesting pose and action, but because she resembled a favorite niece, and hence the title of this picture—a tribute to little "Karen."

Apply Maskoid to preserve the white areas.

PAINTING INSTRUCTIONS FOR KAREN

Size of original painting—10¼ by 13¾ inches. Paper—300-pound D'Arches.

Step 1. After carefully drawing the figure, apply Maskoid to the light portions of water splashed from the sprinkling can. Use an inexpensive brush.

Step 2. The sky is covered with a light wash of Yellow Ochre, using an Aquarelle brush, and while still wet, is overpainted with a very light wash of Cobalt Blue. Using a number 12 brush, lay a wash of Rembrandt Green over the water area. While it is still wet, apply a second wash of Permanent Blue which will blend automatically. Leave paper white for the breaker and continue colors to the shore, using horizontal brush strokes in a free arm movement. While still wet, add Yellow Ochre with the Aquarelle brush, to suggest sand under shallow water in foreground. Use Antwerp Blue and Rembrandt Green for the water from the sprinkling can, painting over the Maskoid on the light areas. The colors are mixed on the paper and applied with a number 8 brush. Allow to dry. Use a very light wash of Lemon Yellow for the flesh and hair. While still wet, apply additional washes of Yellow Ochre and Orange, blended on the

paper with a number 8 brush. Remove the Maskoid when paper is thoroughly dry.

Step 3. Paint shaded flesh areas with Burnt Sienna and Alizarin Crimson, mixed on the palette. Water from sprinkling can is painted with Permanent Blue and Rembrandt Green, mixed on the paper. Darken accents with these colors intensified, using less water. When the paper is dry, darker flesh tones are painted with the same colors as before—Burnt Sienna and Alizarin Crimson—in a series of applications, using a number 8 brush. To create the desired depth and intensity, this was done six times. Intensifying the color gradually in this way eliminates the danger of painting too dark, too soon, and keeps the color fresh. With each application of color, darker areas are modeled into the light, and the paper is allowed to dry thoroughly before the next coat is applied.

Step 4. For the bathing suit use Permanent Blue with a light touch of Indian Red. Mix on the paper, and model while damp. When the paper is dry, darker accents are added with the same colors. The sprinkling can is painted with a light wash of Red and modeled with the addition of Mauve. Soften wave with a bristle brush. (See color plate on page 19.)

MAKE QUICK ACTION SKETCHES
DRAWING FROM THE ARM

CLIP ACTION
SHOTS FROM NEWSPAPERS
AND MAGAZINES AND
MAKE LOOSE PENCIL SKETCHES
FOR PRACTICE

II. THE CHILD IN ACTION

Children are by nature full of life and energy. Because they are usually in a constant state of motion, posing them presents great difficulties. Getting an active child to stand still for any length of time is an arduous task, and his natural spontaneity and charm are generally lost in the process.

The way out of this dilemma is to make quick action-sketches or to take snap-shots with your camera when the child is unaware that he is a model. Either or both can be used as the basis for a painting done without the presence of the model. Notes on color and lighting, made on the spot, are extremely helpful in developing the painting later in the studio.

Capturing physical action in a drawing requires a lot of observation and ingenuity. Much practice is essential to gain speed and proficiency in drawing action sketches. They should be handled in a loose free style. On the following pages are a few examples of such sketches with helpful suggestions on how they were done. Note the use of Basic Forms. The single-line figure is a good aid in catching action, as shown on page 48. Some of the most helpful quick sketches are those that catch a particular detail of an action such as the twist of a child's arms.

The camera, of course, is a great help in securing material, but the big problem is to photograph the child without his knowledge. The natural actions of a child lend themselves to very provocative poses, and if some of these can be captured while the subject is unaware, the results will not be stilted. For example, the action sketches on the following pages were not posed, in contrast to the bottom sketch on page 27. In the latter, note that the face is looking directly into the "camera," and the sketch lacks spontaneity.

Patience and quick action on the part of the photographer can produce extensive material from which action sketches can be made. In photographing a child in action, it is not necessary to get a good picture. In fact, it's almost better if the photograph is not too good so that the danger of copying will be eliminated. Not all cameras are fast enough to stop action, but the data obtained is helpful as a guide from which a freer, more mobile drawing can be made.

Capture spontaneous action in quick pencil sketches.

THE BEACH IS A GOOD PLACE
TO MAKE
ACTION
SKETCHES

TRY FOR PROVACATIVE
POSES

AVOID TOO
MUCH
MUSCLE
STRUCTURE

SO IS THE BEDROOM

getting ready for her bath

DRAW FREELY
USING YOUR ARM

GET THE SPIRIT
OF THE
ACTION

USE A
6B PENCIL

Look for provocative poses.

A THIRSTY YOUNG MAN

and A YOUNG MISS

a little girl with a big broom

LEARN TO DRAW WITH SIMPLE OUTLINES IT WILL HELP YOU WHEN YOU PAINT.

DRAW WITHIN THE SHAPE

FIRST THE SHAPE

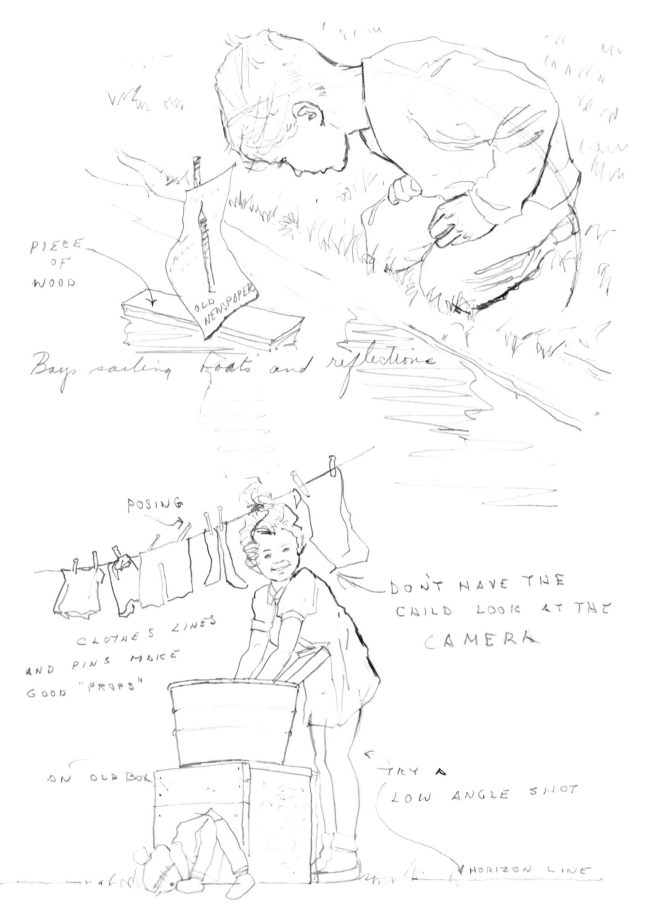

PIECE
OF
WOOD

OLD
NEWSPAPER

Boys sailing boats and reflections

POSING

CLOTHES LINES
AND PINS MAKE
GOOD "PROPS"

DON'T HAVE THE
CHILD LOOK AT THE
CAMERA

AN OLD BOX

TRY A
LOW ANGLE SHOT

HORIZON LINE

THREE HAITIAN GIRLS IN BLUE

The palette for painting the dark skin tones in "Three Haitian Girls in Blue" is a simple one. I used only four colors—Burnt Sienna, Sepia, Permanent Blue, and Black. Various combinations of these colors can produce subtle nuances, avoiding monotony of color. Other colors are used, of course, in the dresses.

The photograph from which this painting was made is another example of an unposed shot. Simple color notes were made on the spot for future use in the studio. I do not work from Kodachromes, nor do I recommend using them because the artist might be tempted to copy the color. This limits his inventive and creative abilities, and usually results in a static painting. In addition, underexposure and overexposure can cause false color and be misleading. Every artist sees color differently and this is one of the things

that makes his work individual. I believe in seeing color through your own eyes rather than through the mechanical means of color film.

The subjects in this painting were walking down a street of Port-au-Prince in gay spirits —no doubt glad that school was over for the day. They obviously were students at a private school whose regulations required the wearing of uniforms. The brilliant blue of their jumpers and their fresh white blouses against their beautiful dark skin was a picture in contrasts.

A bit of trickery was involved in taking this photograph. I focused the camera on my wife who was standing near the children, and when they turned to look at her, I snapped the picture without their knowledge. This is a helpful ruse that we often use. She doesn't get many pictures taken this way, but I get material.

PAINTING INSTRUCTIONS

FOR

THREE HAITIAN GIRLS

IN BLUE

Step 1.   Make a careful drawing.

Size of original painting—10¼ by 13¾ inches. Paper—200-pound Saunders rough Imperial. Brush—number 8 used for all steps.

Step 2.   Apply a wash of Burnt Sienna over all flesh areas and hair. Allow to dry. Cover jumpers and shoes with a wash of Cobalt Blue, and allow to dry. Paint the louvered door in background with a wash of thinly diluted Black. Add Burnt Sienna on the right door panel. Then paint the wall with a wash of light Yellow Ochre, adding and blending light touches of Cadmium Red and Permanent Blue. Continue the wash onto the pavement in foreground using the same colors. When dry, paint darker tones in foreground with a thin wash of Sepia, and blend.

Step 3.   Apply a deeper tone of Burnt Sienna to the flesh areas of right and left figures. Keep your brush damp but not wet. When dry, add Sepia to the shadow areas on the faces and legs, and blend. Paint flesh areas of center figure with the same colors, and when the paper is dry, add Blue. For the shadows on dresses and shoes, use Cobalt Blue, Payne's Grey and Mauve, mixed on the palette. Paint the hair with Black, Sepia, and Burnt Sienna, mixed on the paper.

MOTHER'S HELPER

Children love to make believe they are grown-up and spend much of their time playing at being adults. They often enjoy helping their parents if they are allowed to use adult tools for the task. A child with an oversized object creates a humorous picture that has a great deal of pictorial appeal as well as human interest. When a child uses a toy shovel, for example, he fits the age group to which he belongs, but give him a man-sized shovel and he becomes almost a caricature. We have all laughed at a little boy with a full-size rake or lawn mower, or a little girl sweeping with a large broom.

In trying to depict this type of situation, I had a 7-year-old boy pose for some photographs, using various adult objects. One of these snapshots was the basis for "Mother's Helper." In this case I did not feel it necessary to make color notes nor rough pencil sketches, but a careful drawing was made using, as I always do, the Basic Form as the first step.

A situation such as this is fun to look at and fun to paint.

THE SISTERS

This is one of the few times I have used someone else's photograph as data for a painting. If done too often, it could simply be called the lazy man's way out. Although the practice is not to be entirely condoned because it does not result in a truly original work, neither is it to be completely condemned. It is often the artist's only source of material that is outside his own locale—for instance, "western" material for the "easterner," or water data for the desert dweller. However, it does have limitations, for without some general knowledge of an area, usually acquired through travel, it is difficult to simulate correct local color and atmosphere.

In the case of "The Sisters," it was not a matter of locale. I was intrigued with this photograph because of the lighting and the large decorative sun-hats on the little girls; although no features could be seen, the feminine quality of the hats gave me the feeling that these must be very pretty little girls. It was the subtle quality of inference that made me want to paint them. To me, the picture is more interesting than it would be if the features were visible. The hats tell the story.

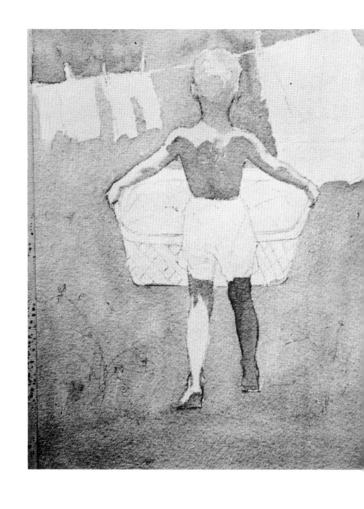

PAINTING INSTRUCTIONS

FOR MOTHER'S HELPER

Step 1. After making a pencil drawing, apply Maskoid over the clothes on line, using a small, inexpensive brush. Paint grassy areas with Hooker's Green, Yellow Ochre, and Burnt Sienna, mixing the colors on the paper with a number 12 brush. Put a wash of Yellow Ochre mixed with touches of Cadmium Red over the figure, and allow to dry. For the shadows on the figure, use Burnt Sienna and Mauve, mixed on the palette. When dry, soften edges with a bristle brush.

Size of original painting—10¼ by 13¾ inches. Paper—300-pound D'Arches.

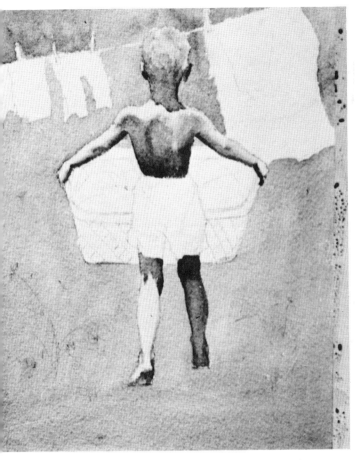 

Step 2. Deepen the darker shadows on the figure with Mauve, Burnt Sienna, and Permanent Blue, mixed on the palette. For the hair, apply a wash of Permanent Blue interspersed with Burnt Sienna, mixing on the paper.

Step 3. For the basket use Permanent Blue and Orange, blended on the paper. (In Rembrandt colors mix Cadmium Yellow Orange and Cadmium Red to get Orange.) Remove Maskoid, and paint the shadows on clothes on line and in basket with Permanent Blue and Yellow Ochre. For the shadows on the boy's shorts, use Yellow Ochre, Orange and Blue, mixed on the paper. Paint the shadows on the grass with Hooker's Green, Lemon Yellow, and Black, mixed on the palette. When the wash over the hair is dry, add touches of Permanent Blue to the highlights. For the dark area, use Black and a touch of Alizarin Crimson, mixed on the palette.

AFTERTHOUGHT: MOTHER'S HELPER

When the painting of "Mother's Helper" was completed, as an afterthought I started to wonder if the addition of some grassy weeds in the foreground might not make it more interesting. Instead of trying this out on acetate as I usually do, I experimented by holding up some live weeds in front of the picture. With my wife's help the painting was photographed with the weeds held in front of it. The hands were then cropped off the picture. You may call this a trick, but it showed the actual effect and proved a point to my satisfaction— that the picture would have been better with the weeds. Do you agree?

PAINTING INSTRUCTIONS FOR THE SISTERS

Step 1.   Make a careful pencil drawing.

Step 2.   Dampen the sky area with a sponge and clean water, and apply a light wash of Yellow Ochre with an Aquarelle brush. While still damp, add a wash of Permanent Blue, making it more intense at the top. When dry, paint the water in the distance with Rembrandt Green and Permanent Blue, again using an Aquarelle brush. Leave the paper white for the crest of the wave. Switch to a number 8 brush and add a touch of Sepia for the darker notes in the under part of the wave. For the foamy water in the foreground, apply Yellow Ochre and a light touch of Permanent Blue, mixed on the paper with very little water; follow the pattern of irregular strokes shown in the painting.

Size of original painting—10¼ by 13¾ inches. Paper—300-pound D'Arches.

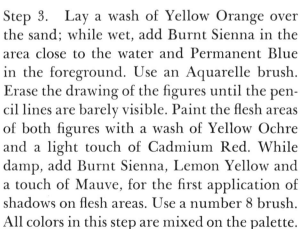

Step 3.   Lay a wash of Yellow Orange over the sand; while wet, add Burnt Sienna in the area close to the water and Permanent Blue in the foreground. Use an Aquarelle brush. Erase the drawing of the figures until the pencil lines are barely visible. Paint the flesh areas of both figures with a wash of Yellow Ochre and a light touch of Cadmium Red. While damp, add Burnt Sienna, Lemon Yellow and a touch of Mauve, for the first application of shadows on flesh areas. Use a number 8 brush. All colors in this step are mixed on the palette.

Step 4.   Paint the hat of the figure on the right with Permanent Blue, Yellow Orange and Cadmium Red. Mix colors on the paper; they will blend automatically. Paint the top of the bathing suit with Yellow Ochre, Permanent Blue and Orange, and the bottom with Yellow Ochre and Antwerp Blue. Deepen shadows on the flesh areas with Mauve, Burnt Sienna, and Lemon Yellow, mixed on the palette, and blend into the underpainting. Use a number 8 brush throughout. Darken the shadowed flesh areas of the figure on the left, using Permanent Blue, Burnt Sienna and Lemon Yellow, mixed on the palette. The hat and bathing suit are Permanent Blue and Orange. Use Payne's Grey and Orange, mixed on the paper, for shadows of the figures on sand, and Payne's Grey and Mauve for the footprints. Pick out the lights on the pebbles with a knife.

AT THE BEACH

This painting of a boy lying prone on the beach was done from a photograph I took while on a raised boardwalk. It was not a posed photo; the subject did not know that I was taking his picture. Seen from the angle of the boardwalk, he appeared to be about sixteen years old. But when he rose, I was quite surprised to notice that he actually was only about ten. My bird's-eye view had elongated the reclining figure and made the boy appear older than he really was. This is a good example of the dangers and subtleties involved in taking a photo or making a drawing from various eye levels. When this type of distortion is intentional, it can add drama.

Taking the photo from this angle placed the subject on a blanket of sand with no water visible. The decorative patterns in the sand make a simple background, and because of its simplicity, the figure dominates the picture. However, the beach background is an important element. This picture serves as a valuable lesson in the palette used to depict sun-tanned flesh.

41

PAINTING INSTRUCTIONS FOR AT THE BEACH

Size of original painting—10¼ by 13¾ inches. Paper—300-pound D'Arches.

Step. 1. Draw the figure carefully, and then erase drawing until hardly visible. Paint the sand in a diagonal direction with thin washes of Yellow Ochre, Sepia, Orange, and Burnt Sienna, mixed on the paper. Use a number 12 brush.

Step 2. Use the same colors intensified for darker tones of the footprints and sand irregularities.

Step 3. Paint the head and figure, except the bathing trunks, with a thin wash of Yellow Ochre and Burnt Sienna, mixed on the palette. While still damp, accent with Indian Red and Burnt Sienna, using a number 8 brush. Allow the paper to dry.

Step 4. For the hair, mix Sepia, Burnt Sienna, Permanent Blue, and Indian Red, on the paper, leaving the underpainting of Yellow Ochre and Burnt Sienna for the light spot on the crown. Do not keep the brush too wet. The darker accents on the arms and body are Indian Red and Sepia, mixed on the palette. Using a number 8 brush, paint the middle tones in the back with Indian Red and Sepia, mixed on the palette, and continue modeling the legs with these colors. When dry, soften the edges with a damp number 8 brush. The shadows on the white bathing trunks are painted with Permanent Blue and Orange, mixed on the paper. Soften the hard edges of the trunks with a bristle brush. Add shadows on the towel with Yellow Ochre, and a touch of Permanent Blue, mixed on the paper.

Catch fluid movement in wash sketches.

BEGINNERS SHOULD USE
THE BASIC FORM
BEFORE PAINTING

WORK FROM
PHOTOGRAPHS AT FIRST

DON'T WORRY
ABOUT
MISTAKES

KEEP YOUR EYES HALF CLOSED
IT WILL HELP YOU TO SEE FORM

KEEP
HAIR
SHAGGY.

SIMPLE
MODELING WHILE
DAMP WILL
GIVE A SOFT
EFFECT

TRY
ADDING A
LINE OR TWO

FOR A SIX INCH
FIGURE USE A
NO. 8 BRUSH

I USE THIS METHOD
TO "PEOPLE" MY
LANDSCAPES
NO 2
BRUSH

R.W.S 140LB PAPER

Try for the particular detail of action—the gesture as well as the posture.

CHILDREN'S NOSES
ARE SMALL

USE SIMPLE LINES
FOR DIRECTION OF HAIR

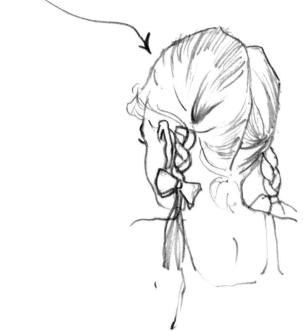

NOTE AXIS
FOR PULL OF
WRINKLES

ADD SHOES OR
FOR
"PROPS"

DOLL

Stop motion—from the single-line figure.

NOTE THIS LINE

The single line figure is a good aid to get action in a hurry

Free action—with pen and ink.

drawing with a pen will help loosen you up

CAN'T DRAW A
STRAIGHT LINE

NOTE
ACTION
LINES

ACTION SKETCHES – HOLD PEN LOOSELY

FREEDOM
IN FOLDS

UPWARD
ACTION

THIS WAS
A SPLATTER – MY PEN
WAS MOVING SWIFTLY
AND STUCK. DON'T STOP –
KEEP GOING

TEST YOUR
PEN

III. PORTRAITURE

The principal concern of the artist in painting a portrait is creating a likeness. However, there is a great deal more to portraiture than this or the portrait painter would have been replaced long ago by the photographer. But a likeness is the starting point.

In catching the essence of individual personality, the child as a subject presents an even greater challenge than the adult. The adult possesses the visible evidences of character and temperament; the child is more unformed, his features softer and his coloring more delicate. It is these soft, tender, fragile qualities of the child—above and beyond a likeness—that the artist strives to capture on paper.

To my mind, watercolor has certain advantages over other mediums in painting portraits of children. The fresh color, with the minimum of overpainting, seems in key with the coloring of the child. However, watercolor has certain limitations in this field—the main one being the size of the head that can be painted. In order to control the color, my suggestion is to paint the head no larger than half of life-size. A very accurate likeness must be achieved in the pencil drawing and no painting should be started until this has been accomplished.

In establishing a pose to work from, it is almost essential to use a photograph. Because of the natural restlessness of children, it is extremely difficult to get a child to "sit" for a portrait. Moreover, the sitter would soon lose his sparkle and spontaneity. So the camera is of tremendous help, although a photograph must not be followed too literally. Individual characteristics and coloring must be carefully observed and studied. Written notes are also helpful.

DRAWING THE HEAD

In drawing the head of the child, the proportion of the face to the head is all-important. A basic rule to remember is that the younger the child, the less head area the features occupy. For example, in the drawings on the facing page, notice that the baby's features are placed low in the head and occupy only about one-third of the head area. The eyes are comparatively large, while the nose and mouth are small. In the 4- to 6-year-old boy, the face is less than half of the head area, while in the 10-year-old girl the face occupies just about half of the head area.

In the diagrammatic drawing of a baby's head on page 54, the Basic Form is almost square; it is divided horizontally into three almost equal parts and vertically in two. The lower third is then divided into four parts. These guide lines are used to determine the placement of the features. Notice that the guide lines in the drawing are curved, giving the head a slightly tilted position. Close-up drawings of individual features built up from their Basic Forms are also shown.

In the diagrammatic drawing of a six-year-old girl on page 55, the Basic Form is rectangular. As this is a head-on view, the guide lines are straight. For placement of the features, the rectangle is divided horizontally into four almost equal sections and vertically in two.

Notice that the features now cover just under half of the face area. As the child grows older, the features continue to "move up" and there is less brow. The eyes become relatively smaller, the nose longer, and the mouth larger; the typical "baby face" disappears.

The use of guide lines is most helpful to the beginner striving for a likeness. They pinpoint errors in drawing such as incorrectly placed features. By studying the subject's features in relation to the lines, individual variations become apparent. Perhaps an eyebrow, or one side of the mouth should be higher than the other—a fact that may otherwise have been overlooked, and that makes a great difference in getting a likeness. A mirror is also a valuable aid in seeing the drawing accurately and in correcting errors.

The preliminary steps or "carpenter work" in constructing a head can be done on layout tissue. When the drawing is satisfactorily completed, contour and features can be traced on watercolor paper. This keeps the drawing clean and eliminates excessive erasing on the paper. It is possible to portray the softness of a child in a drawing, if it is done very skillfully. However, when painting in watercolor, the drawing is merely a foundation upon which the artist works to fully realize his goal of a soft, delicate painting.

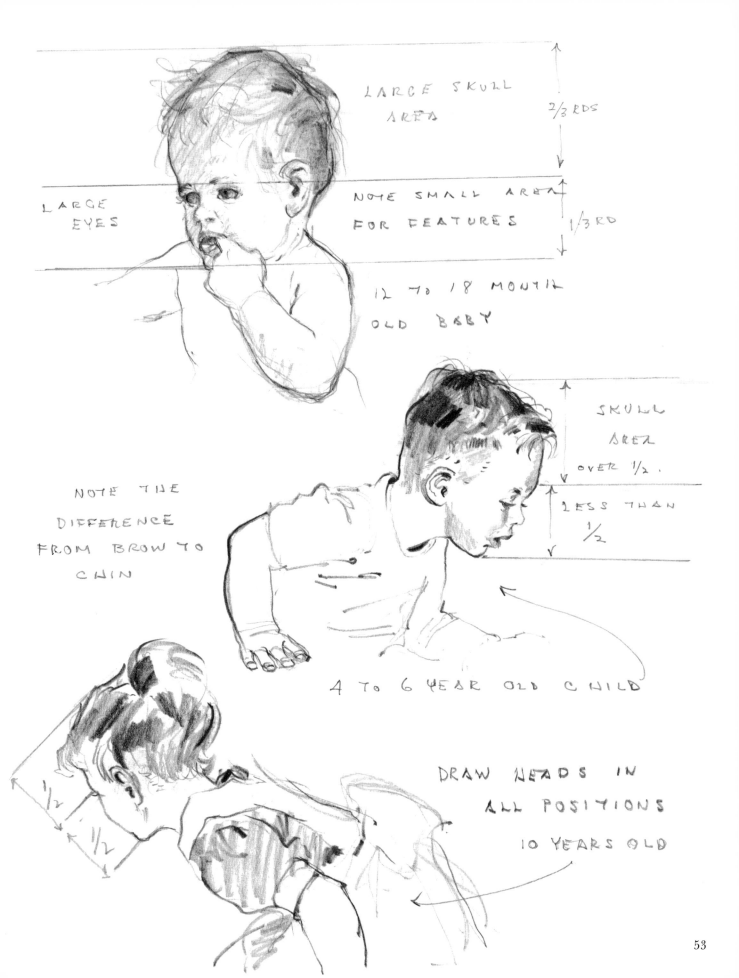

LARGE SKULL
AREA

2/3 RDS

LARGE
EYES

NOTE SMALL AREA
FOR FEATURES

1/3 RD

12 TO 18 MONTH
OLD BABY

SKULL
AREA
OVER 1/2.

LESS THAN
1/2

NOTE THE
DIFFERENCE
FROM BROW TO
CHIN

4 TO 6 YEAR OLD CHILD

1/2

1/2

DRAW HEADS IN
ALL POSITIONS

10 YEARS OLD

Use guide lines for placement of features.

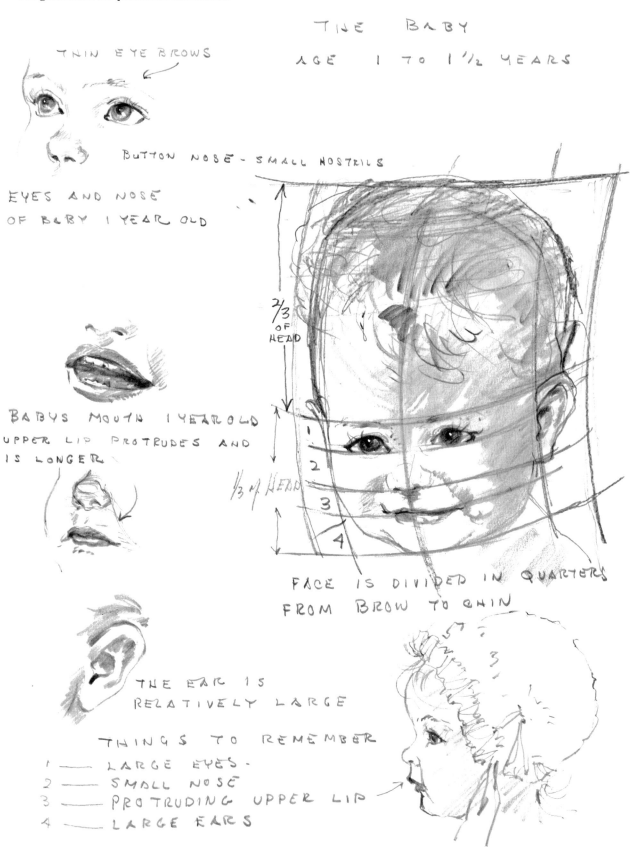

THIN EYE BROWS

BUTTON NOSE - SMALL NOSTRILS

EYES AND NOSE
OF BABY 1 YEAR OLD

THE BABY
AGE 1 TO 1½ YEARS

2/3 OF HEAD

⅓ OF HEAD

1
2
3
4

BABYS MOUTH 1 YEAR OLD

UPPER LIP PROTRUDES AND
IS LONGER

FACE IS DIVIDED IN QUARTERS
FROM BROW TO CHIN

THE EAR IS
RELATIVELY LARGE

THINGS TO REMEMBER

1 ——— LARGE EYES.
2 ——— SMALL NOSE
3 ——— PROTRUDING UPPER LIP
4 ——— LARGE EARS

THE CHILD — 5 - 9 YEARS

→ FACE IS DIVIDED IN HALF

HORIZONTAL LINES WILL
KEEP FEATURES IN LINE

EYES SMALLER IN
PROPORTION TO THE HEAD

EARS SLIGHTLY SMALLER

NOSE LONGER

MOUTH LARGER

THIS CHILD IS 6 YEARS OLD

THE EYE (LEFT)

1. — BASIC FORM

2. — ROUND THE EDGES

3. — THEN MODEL

THE EAR

1 — BASIC SHAPE

2 — DRAW THE FORM

3 — THEN MODEL

THE LIPS

— 1 BASIC FORM

— 2 DIVIDE IN HALF

— 3 MODEL

KEEP DRAWING
PARTS !

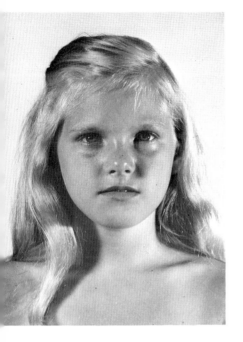 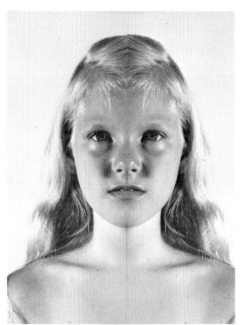 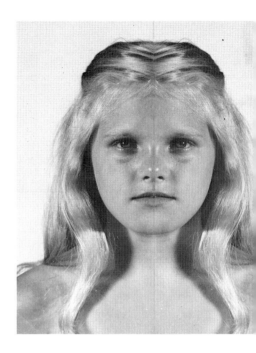

ASYMMETRY OF THE FACE

Because no face is exactly the same on both sides, the artist should not try for perfect symmetry of features. If he does, he will not get the individual characteristics that are essential in making a likeness. The photographs shown here demonstrate this point; the composite photographs were made by cutting the original in half, and then duplicating and joining each half. Note the unnatural look of the composite photographs as compared to the original.

HAIR STYLES

A becoming hair style can greatly improve the appearance of even a little girl. Any style is in fashion as long as it is becoming and appropriate to the age of the child. Notice that some hair styles, such as the "biscuit" shown in the photograph on this page, add years to a child's age.

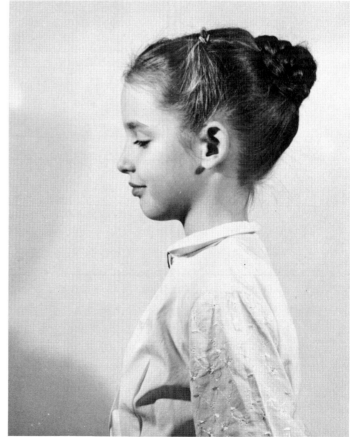

PAINTING THE HEAD: SUSAN

Susan was chosen for this demonstration because I felt she typified the average American child. Inasmuch as my objective was to do a step-by-step demonstration showing the technique of painting a head, I was not overly concerned with composition, mood, or likeness.

The drawing was made from the photograph shown here. In order to include as much detail as possible in this demonstration, the painting was done in eight steps, and each step was photographed as soon as it was completed. From the viewpoint of the artist, stopping for photographs is not an ideal ar-rangement but the photographic record of each stage is helpful in showing the building of the head in color and form. This accurate record of the progress of the painting was made possible by skillful color photography.

I have used a simplified palette for those who have only limited experience in painting the head. For the flesh tones, only the following five colors are used: Lemon Yellow, Burnt Sienna, Cadmium Red, Alizarin Crimson, and Mauve; for the eyes, Permanent Blue and Sepia; for the hair, Indian Red, Hooker's Green, Burnt Umber, and Lemon Yellow.

Step 1

Step 2

SUSAN

Step 5

Step 6

Step 3

Step 4

A painting demonstration in color. See following pages for instructions.

Step 7

Step 8

PAINTING INSTRUCTIONS FOR SUSAN

Size of original painting—10 x 12 inches.   Paper—400-pound Royal Watercolor Society.

See pages 60 and 61 for these painting steps in color.

Step 1.   Throw a light wash of Lemon Yellow mixed with Burnt Sienna on the head (except the eyes and teeth), and while wet, add a light touch of Cadmium Red on the cheeks.

Step 2.   When dry, put on a second wash of Lemon Yellow and Burnt Sienna for the first stage of modeling. Soften with a sable brush.

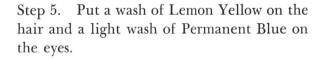

Step 5.   Put a wash of Lemon Yellow on the hair and a light wash of Permanent Blue on the eyes.

Step 6.   For the eyebrows use Burnt Sienna, Lemon Yellow, Burnt Umber, and Mauve. Darken blue of eyes with Sepia and Permanent Blue.

Use a number 8 brush and mix all colors on the palette. Allow paper to dry after each step.

Step 3. Continue modeling, using the same colors with the addition of Mauve. Soften edges.

Step 4. Paint the lips with Cadmium Red, and Alizarin Crimson, using Mauve for accents. Continue deepening tones on head with original colors.

Step 7. For darks in the hair use Burnt Sienna, Hooker's Green, Lemon Yellow, along with a touch of Sepia and Indian Red.

Step 8. Apply a final wash of Alizarin Crimson over the entire face, except the eyes and teeth. Then continue to model with Lemon Yellow, Burnt Sienna, and Mauve until finished.

A FEW MOODS

GLOOM

FROWN

HAPPY

TO

GLEE

EXPRESSIONS

Children usually express their feelings very directly; they have not acquired the adult skill of hiding emotions. In general, the face of a child is more mobile and expressive than the face of an adult.

The eyes, eyebrows, and mouth are very important in depicting expression as is shown in the series of heads on this page. I had a little fun with this old cartoonist trick—first drawing the head, and then with a tissue overlay, gradually changing the expression from gloom to glee with a few strokes. It may suggest ways of experimenting and practicing. The sketches on the facing page illustrate some typical expressions of children.

A FEW ROUGHS - SKETCHES
FOR VARIOUS EXPRESSIONS

6 YEARS
OLD

pensive
doubt

BIG
DARK EYES

Sadness   2 YEARS
Hunger   OLD

3 YEARS
OLD

Carefree
Happy

Surprise
expecting

10 YEARS
OLD

65

MODELLING
WITHOUT
LINE

1 2 3

1ST
VALUE

2ND
VALUE

3RD VALUE

TRY WORKING
IN 3 VALUES
1-LIGHT
2-MEDIUM
3-DARK
I USED A.W.S. 300LB PAPER

WORK FROM LIGHT
TO DARK OVER THIN
PENCIL DRAWING

THE PORTRAIT

IN MONOCHROME WATERCOLOR

Monochrome watercolor is a most effective medium for portraiture. The artist works in different values of a single color such as sepia, black, and so forth.

In painting a one-color wash drawing, I start with a thin pencil drawing and work from light to dark as shown in the sketch of

the baby's head. I used three values—light, medium and dark—in modeling the little girl's head. These two wash drawings represent preliminary stages in painting a portrait in monochrome watercolor. The illustration on the facing page is an example of a finished portrait in this medium.

MODELLING OVER LINE

SIMPLE DIRECT
WASHES USING A FLAT BRUSH FOR
FIRST WASHES
FINISH WITH POINTED BRUSH

THE PORTRAIT IN LINE AND WASH

Watercolor used in a linear manner may be combined with wash as in the illustrations shown here and on the facing page. For the head of the boy, the line drawing was done first and then the head was modeled with the wash. In contrast, the head of the girl is an example of line drawing over wash. The flat wash was applied first and allowed to dry. The head was painted quite dry over the wash with a worn brush to produce a loose, sketchy effect. The worn end of a brush handle is often used for this purpose. The first method —wash over line—is used more widely for commercial work than for portraits.

Kirsti Olsen

PORTRAITS:

PEN AND INK AND LITHOGRAPH PENCIL

The portraits reproduced here and on the facing page—two in pen and ink and one in lithograph pencil—illustrate two different methods of drawing. As in painting with a brush, the handling of the pen or pencil determines the type of line produced and the looseness or tightness of the finished work.

The pen-and-ink drawing of the girl and the dog was drawn with the pen held as for writing, between the thumb and index finger,

as shown in the accompanying photograph. The lithograph pencil was held in the same way for the lithograph pencil sketch.

In contrast, the pen and ink drawing of the girl's head was drawn with a loose arm movement. The pen was held well back from the point with the end in the palm as shown in the accompanying photograph. This produced a soft, feathery effect—quite different from the tighter, harder lines of the other two drawings.

THINK IN TERMS
OF PAINTING

KEEP EDGES
IRREGULAR FOR
SOFTNESS →

I USED A
CROQUILL PEN
ON
STRATHMORE
PAPER

DO NOT OVER MODEL
KEEP IT SIMPLE!

I USED A
CROQUILL PEN
ON
STRATHMORE
PAPER

PORTRAIT OF A GIRL AND HER DOLL

In planning this demonstration of the steps in painting a portrait, I tried to keep the pose as simple as possible, and at the same time to create a picture that expressed the mood and feeling of childhood.

Rocking a doll to sleep is a very real part of a little girl's world of make-believe. The tender maternal quality of this little girl's expression as she lovingly holds her doll in her lap is one of the things I have tried to capture. It is typical of what I mean by the essence of the child's personality—over and

above a photographic likeness. The night scene suggested by the pose enhances the mood and serves as a simple background for the child.

The preliminary ideas are shown on the following pages; they include pencil roughs, wash sketches, a color sketch (reproduced in black and white) that served as a color guide, and the final drawing. The painting steps were recorded by color photography and are reproduced on page 80. The finished painting appears as the frontispiece.

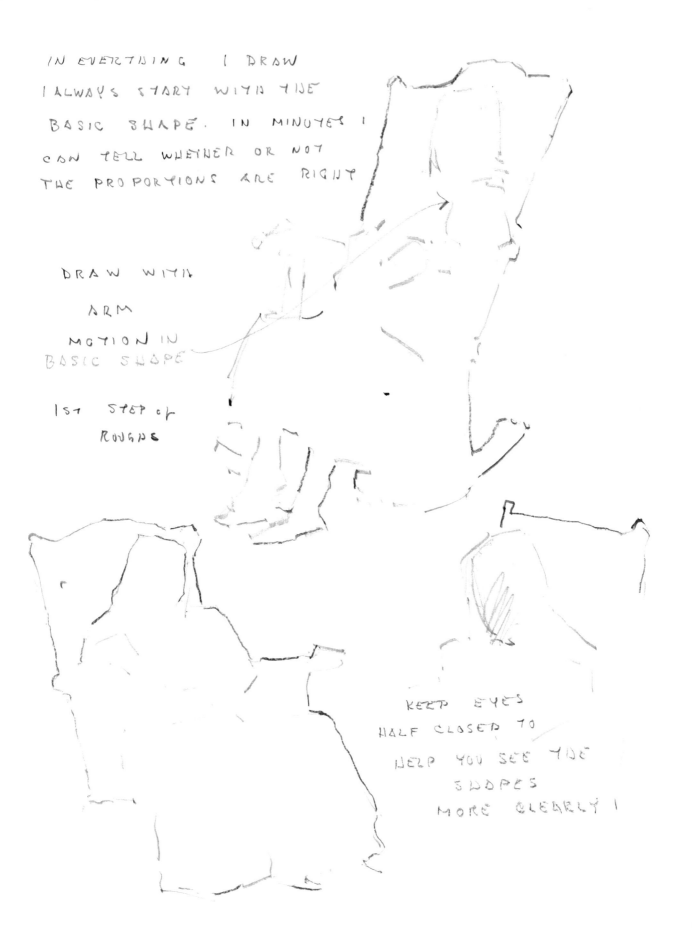

IN EVERTHING I DRAW
I ALWAYS STARY WITH THE
BASIC SHAPE. IN MINUTES I
CAN TELL WHETHER OR NOT
THE PROPORTIONS ARE RIGHT

DRAW WITH
    ARM
    MOTION IN
BASIC SHAPE

IST STEP of
    ROUGHS

KEEP EYES
HALF CLOSED TO
HELP YOU SEE THE
    SHAPES
MORE CLEARLY!

Become familiar with your subject.

ON THE PRELIMINARY ROUGHS TRY
MAINLY FOR ACTION AND — IN THIS
CASE MOTION

GRADUALLY
BUILD UP TO

YOUR FINAL

DRAWING

DRAW
THESE
ROUGHS
WITH
ARM
MOTION

SECOND STEP (ROUGHS)

DIRECTION OF
LIGHT

FLANNEL
NIGHT GOWN

POSITION of
DOLL

3RD STEP (ROUGHS

Do not overpaint wash sketches—spontaneity will be lost.

wash sketches will help with lighting

AND ALSO
"LOOSEN YOU UP"

She begins to look like a madonna

PAINT "DIRECT"
DO NOT OVERPAINT
THE SPONTANEITY WILL
BE LOST

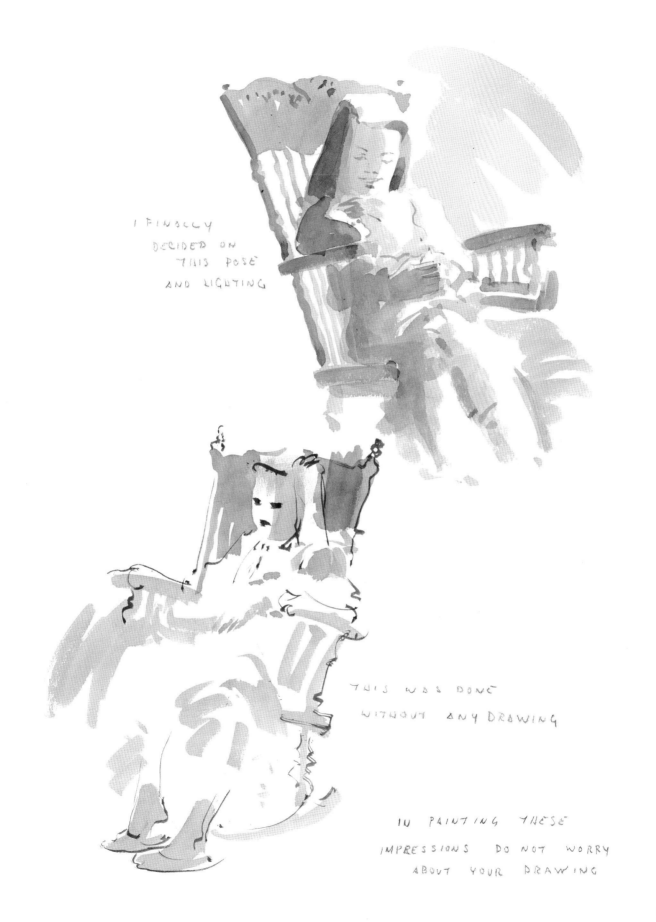

I FINALLY
DECIDED ON
THIS POSE
AND LIGHTING

THIS WAS DONE
WITHOUT ANY DRAWING

IN PAINTING THESE
IMPRESSIONS DO NOT WORRY
ABOUT YOUR DRAWING

This preliminary color sketch reproduced in black and white was the color guide for "Portrait of a Girl and Her Doll." The pencil drawing shown on the facing page served as the base for the painting.

PORTRAIT OF A GIRL AND HER DOLL

Step 1

Step 2

Step 3

Step 4

A painting demonstration in color. The finished portrait appears as the frontispiece.

PAINTING INSTRUCTIONS

Size of original painting—10 x 12 inches.
Paper—300-pound D'Arches.

Step 1. Paint the background, including chair, with Antwerp Blue, Sepia, Burnt Sienna, Yellow Orange, and Permanent Blue, mixed on the paper and blended, using a 2-inch brush. While wet, add shadows to the girl's dress with an Aquarelle brush, applying Permanent Blue and Orange, mixed on the paper. Paint the hair, except the white part where light is striking, with Lemon Yellow and Yellow Ochre using a number 8 brush. While wet, add Hooker's Green and Sepia to the shaded area, and allow to dry.

Step 2. Lay a wash of Yellow Ochre, Yellow Orange, and Cadmium Red thinly mixed on the palette, over the head and hands, and the doll's face and legs, using an Aquarelle brush. While wet, wipe the left side of the forehead with a damp Aquarelle brush to create a highlight. When dry, intensify the hands with a second wash of the same colors. While the head area is wet, add a touch of Cadmium Red to the cheeks using an Aquarelle brush. For the chair, use Sepia, Burnt Sienna, Permanent Blue, Indian Red, and Antwerp Blue, mixed on the paper. Use a number 12 brush, painting loosely with an arm movement.

Step 3. When dry, continue painting the head with a number 8 brush. Mix Yellow Ochre, Orange (in Rembrandt Colors, Cadmium Red and Yellow Orange produce Orange), and Hooker's Green on the palette, and apply to all shaded areas of the face. Soften edges with the same brush. Continue applying colors until desired depth is reached. Allow to dry between each application. For the hair apply a medium wash of Lemon Yellow with a touch of Medium Yellow, mixed on the palette. Leave out white area. Paint the back of the chair and the arm-rest with Antwerp Blue, Sepia, and Burnt Sienna, using an Aquarelle brush and mixing the color on the paper. Use the same colors applied with a number 8 brush for the rungs. While wet, pat out some of the color on the chair arm with a blotter to bring out the undercoating. Allow to dry.

Step 4. Use number 8 brush throughout this step. Add Burnt Sienna and Sepia, mixed on paper, to dark part of the hair, ending up at shoulder line with Permanent Blue and Sepia. Add Cadmium Red to the cheek in shadow and soften with same brush. With the edge of a blotter pull out light streaks in hair on right side near face. Add a light note of Yellow Ochre to teeth, and then a light tint of Permanent Blue over Ochre. Let dry. Paint the eyebrows with Hooker's Green, Sepia, and Indian Red, mixed on palette, and soften. For the doll's legs, use Lemon Yellow, Alizarin Crimson and Mauve, mixed thinly on paper. Deepen the chair, using the same colors as before—Antwerp Blue, Sepia, and Burnt Sienna—mixed on the paper.

Step 5. (See frontispiece.) Darken head, using a number 8 brush and the same colors as in Step 1. Soften after each application of color. With a clean sponge, wipe out color in nightgown, taking care to clean sponge thoroughly after each stroke with clean water so as to avoid reapplying color. For dark accents of corners of mouth, apply Mauve with a number 2 brush. Deepen chair with the same three colors, mixed on the paper.

MASKOID   MASKOID   MASK.

PAINT
REFLECTIONS
HORIZONTALLY

WET SAND

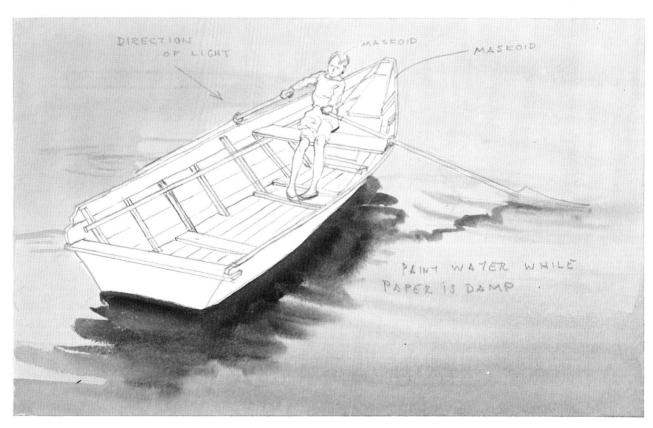

DIRECTION
OF LIGHT   MASKOID   MASKOID

PAINT WATER WHILE
PAPER IS DAMP .

IV. THE CHILD

IN HIS OWN ENVIRONMENT

The part that backgrounds play in painting children depends on whether the goal is a formal portrait or a picture with the figure of a child in it. When the main concern of the artist is a likeness, the background plays a minor role, for it is usually only a simple backdrop for setting off the figure. But when the background is an integral part of the picture, it is as important as the figure.

The background may emphasize the feeling and mood of childhood. It may show the child in a typical setting—one that is representative of his activities and interests.

Since many of the child's activities are conducted outdoors, a background of nature is a particularly appropriate setting. As examples of this, I used the beach as the setting for "Karen," "The Sisters," and "Comaraderie"; and the river for "The Young Fisherman."

The addition of the figure of a child in the right setting can "make" a picture, give it universal appeal, and sometimes even add a humorous note.

Detail of "The Waif." The painting
is shown in color on page 88.

THE WAIF

Although this painting was not done "on
location" it is authentic, for it is a composite
of data observed and photographed while on
a visit to Haiti. The fascinating shapes and
textures of the building first stimulated my
desire to paint it. However, when I started the
painting I felt that the design of the picture
required a figure. Since the photograph of the
building did not include a figure, I turned
to a combination of memory and other Haitian photos to provide a model. As the painting progressed, the small figure of the boy
against the heavy structure of the building
established the mood of the painting. He
is typical of the sad, undernourished Haitian boys we saw during our visit—a heart-
breaking commentary on the devastation of
drought and consequent food shortage.

Sketches of the preliminary "thinking" and
"planning" stages are shown on the following
pages. Both the figure and the background
show the use of abstract forms and basic
shapes in planning the composition. Inasmuch as this picture was painted for exhibi-
tion, there are no painting instructions. It is
included in this book as an example of the
importance of backgrounds in relationship to
a figure.

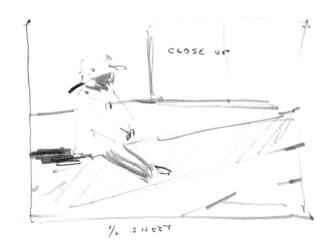

CLOSE UP

½ SHEET

THINKING STAGE

FULL SHEET

I ALWAYS
START WITH
THE
ABSTRACT
SHAPE

LONG + NARROW

FULL SHEET WITH TOP CUT TO MAKE A HORIZONTAL SHAPE

IN THESE SKETCHES I WAS LOOKING FOR THE SHAPE OF
THE PICTURE AND FIGURE PLACEMENT

Develop the final pose and composition from rough sketches.

THIS POSE

Preliminary
sketches

Hands

and

legs

AND DETAILS

GETTING ACQUAINTED WITH THE ACTION, I MADE
SEVERAL SKETCHES. NOTE ELIMINATION OF DETAIL

DEVELOPING STAGE

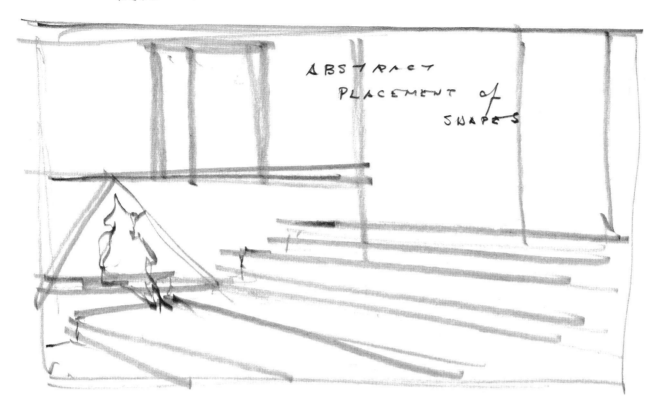

ABSTRACT
PLACEMENT of
SHAPES

FINAL SKETCH

I finally decided on the full sheet
see finished painting on P. 89 -

THE WAIF

In my opinion, of all the backgrounds used in this book, this one presents the strongest argument for the important part they play in setting the stage for the subject. I'd like to quote the reaction of a writer-friend of mine upon seeing this picture: "The big, strong, blocky shapes give the picture strength; the small, frail, pensive child against this background and in contrast to it, give it drama. Neither the figure nor the background would be nearly so interesting without the other."

THE YOUNG FISHERMAN

Many contemporary painters would not consider painting a scene such as this. But if scenes reminiscent of traditional childhood are not acceptable to all, they still hold fascination for many, including myself.

Perhaps the background in this painting assumes greater importance than the figure, but the figure, a boy engaged in a typical youngster's activity, is still the center of interest and the painting is enhanced by it. The combination has created a nostalgic picture rather than just a painting of a child, or a river scene. Roughs appear on page 90.

Make painting notes on your rough sketches.

PAINTING INSTRUCTIONS

FOR THE YOUNG FISHERMAN

Size of original painting—18 x 24 inches.
Paper—300-pound D'Arches.

Step 1. Make a careful drawing. Maskoid hands and hat of figure, and exposed roots of trees.

Step 2. Paint background of river bank with Burnt Sienna, Sepia, Hooker's Green, and Yellow Ochre, mixing colors on the paper and blending. Use a number 8 brush. Apply Hooker's Green, Yellow Ochre, and Orange, mixed on the paper, to the grassy area on the river bank in foreground. Use an Aquarelle brush. For the trees use Sepia, Burnt Sienna, Black, and Permanent Blue, mixed on the paper with a 3/4-inch flat brush. When dry, deepen with the same colors. Paint the shadows on the grass with Lemon Yellow and Black, mixed on palette. Use a number 8 brush. For the clay river bank paint over Maskoided roots with Burnt Sienna, Sepia, Permanent Blue, mixed on paper. When this is dry, remove Maskoid, and intensify values using the same colors.

Step. 3. Use a number 8 brush throughout this step. Paint the face with Burnt Sienna and Lemon Yellow, mixed on the palette. When Maskoid is dry remove it from the hands and hat; paint the hands using same colors. Leave light on hand as shown in the painting. For the remainder of this step the colors are mixed on the paper. Paint the shadow of the hat with Orange, Permanent Blue and a touch of Yellow Ochre. Paint the overalls with a wash of Payne's Grey, Permanent Blue and Black. When dry, deepen with the same colors. Use Red and Mauve for the shirt, intensifying these colors for shadow and darker accents. Soften edges with 1/4-inch bristle brush.

Step 4. Put a thin wash of Antwerp Blue over the river area and, while it is still wet, add Burnt Sienna as shown in the finished painting. Add Yellow Ochre and Sepia to foreground. When the paper is dry, paint the reflections in the water with a 3/4-inch flat brush working in horizontal brush strokes. The colors are mixed on the palette—Hooker's Green, Burnt Sienna, and Sepia for the reflections in background; Permanent Blue, Black, and Payne's Grey for the reflection of boy; Sepia, Black, Burnt Sienna, Burnt Umber for the reflections of trees.

Step 5. When the paper is thoroughly dry, paint the background water including the reflections, using Antwerp Blue, Rembrandt Green, and Cobalt Blue. Work in horizontal brush strokes with an Aquarelle brush. From the point where the figure is standing to the foreground, use darker notes of the same colors. Add Sepia and Yellow Ochre to the extreme foreground, again painting over the reflections. With a bristle brush lift out ripples in water next to the fishline.

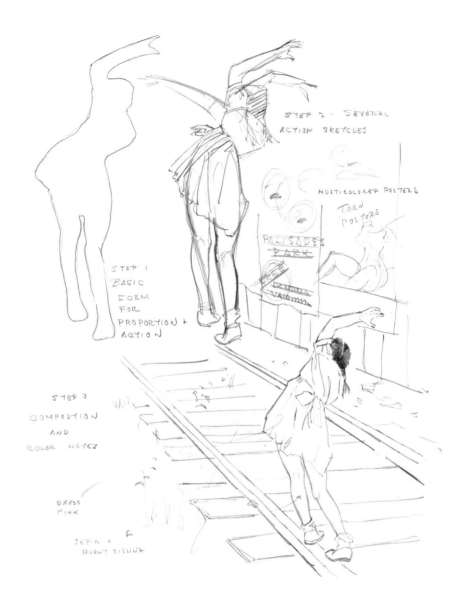

The figure is labeled with handwritten notes:

STEP 2 - SEVERAL ACTION SKETCHES

MULTICOLORED POSTERS

TORN POSTERS

PALISADES PARK

STEP 1 BASIC FORM FOR PROPORTION + ACTION

STEP 3 COMPOSITION AND COLOR NOTES

DRESS PINK

SEPIA + BURNT SIENNA

THE TIGHTROPE WALKER

The setting for the child in "The Tightrope Walker" presented a problem that took months of experimentation to solve. This is a strong example of how important backgrounds are to me. The starting point in this case was an intriguing photograph (of rather poor quality) of a child walking the tracks— a typical youngster's pastime. The background, a rural country scene, was changed in the drawing stage to a harbor cove with boats, as shown in the pencil sketch on page 94. Both these settings seemed unsatisfactory. The poster background finally chosen was taken from material I photographed in New York. It brought to mind the circus, and immediately suggested a proper setting for the figure. This background placed the child in a world of fantasy, and at the same time tied the picture together and suggested the title.

This harbor background was discarded.

PAINTING INSTRUCTIONS

FOR THE TIGHTROPE WALKER

Size of original painting—22 by 30 inches. Paper—300-pound D'Arches.

Step 1.   Make a careful drawing, after blocking out the Basic Form.

Step 2.   Lay a thin wash of Burnt Sienna over the arms and legs with a number 8 brush. When the paper is dry, mix a very thin wash of Alizarin Crimson and Crimson Red on the palette, and apply over the dress. For the background, put a thin wash of Black over the entire picture, except the figure, the tops of the rails, and the whites in the posters. Use an Aquarelle brush.

Step 3.   Darken the arms and legs with Sepia and a touch of Permanent Blue, mixed on the palette, using a number 8 brush. For the hair, use Black, Burnt Sienna and Permanent Blue, mixed on the paper. While still wet, "push" the colors together to blend them. For the dark tones in the dress, add Mauve and Alizarin Crimson, mixed on the palette.

Step 4.   Cover the socks with a thin wash of Orange, Permanent Blue and Burnt Sienna, mixed on the paper. Use Burnt Sienna and Orange for the shoes. When the paper is dry, add Sepia for dark tones. Accent the socks with Orange and Blue.

Step 5.   For the posters, use the full range of the palette, as suggested in the finished painting. Apply a second thin wash of Black over the entire area of the fence and railroad ties except the figure, posters and highlights on the rails. While the paper is still damp, add light touches of Burnt Sienna, Blue, and Sepia. Use an Aquarelle brush. When dry, accent the boards and ties with deep notes of Sepia and Burnt Sienna, using a fan brush to create texture.

Step 6.   Paint in stones with Burnt Sienna, Black and Sepia, using a number 8 brush. When the paper is dry, nick out highlights with a razor. For the grasses, apply Yellow Ochre, Burnt Sienna, and Sepia with a fan brush.

Step 7.   Use Permanent Blue, Burnt Sienna, Sepia, and Orange for the shadows of the figure on the tracks. For the shadows of the rails, use Permanent Blue, Burnt Sienna, and Sepia.

CROPPING A PICTURE

This painting didn't quite come off as I had expected; my original idea was to paint the little boy stealing apples, but somehow he got lost in the busy street scene. In an effort to salvage the original idea, I experimented by cropping the picture—first the top and foreground, and then all four sides. I finally eliminated all but the boy and the fruit stand with the three passing figures in front of it.

This simple process has saved many a painting for me. From it I have learned not to discard a seemingly unsuccessful painting before determining whether it can be salvaged or used as data for another painting.

THE SIMPLE FIGURE

The composition of a landscape often calls for the addition of a small figure or group of figures. The figure can enhance the mood of the painting, give it drama or human interest. Since such figures are comparatively small (about 1 to 1-½ inches in a painting 20 by 28 inches), they can be executed very simply. No preliminary drawing is necessary and the painting is done in five or six quick strokes.

The accompanying illustration shows the steps in painting the figures of the three little girls in "Aspetuck Corners," shown on the facing page. Note that the girls' dresses have been left white. The figures were painted with a number 5 brush.

The detail of the painting shows the actual size of the figures and the crudeness of the painting. In the picture itself, however, the lack of structure is not apparent and the figures have become a part of the landscape.

1   2   3   4

ACETATE   Sometimes a painting may be improved by adding figures, a house, or trees. It is helpful to first test the effect by painting on acetate placed over the picture. Acetate, a celluloid-like material manufactured by DuPont, is available in transparent sheets that can be painted on, washed clean and then used over again. This simple device has saved many paintings.

A demonstration of painting on acetate is shown in the accompanying illustrations. Do you think that the picture is improved with the figure added? I preferred it without. By trying out the change on acetate, I saved myself the work of deleting the figure.

Technically, casein is considered a watercolor medium because water is the solvent used. But contrary to watercolor painting, opaque white is used extensively with casein and produces the mat finish usually associated with it. Although casein is occasionally used transparently without opaque white, in my opinion, casein has no advantages over watercolor when used in this way and does not have its clear brilliance.

However, in painting a portrait, casein does have certain advantages, for color can be washed off and the area repainted–provided that it has not been allowed to dry too thoroughly. When completely dry it is impervious to all solvents. There are many fine painters who prefer to work in casein above all mediums. And I will admit a preference for casein over oil for painting portraits of children, but since I am a watercolorist at heart, I remain partial and loyal to watercolor. Nevertheless, I have included one example of a casein painting in this book for those who do not feel as strongly as I do on this subject.

My casein palette setup is very much the same as for watercolor with the colors arranged from warm to cool. I use Shiva colors and again this is a matter of a personal preference, not superior quality. The warm colors are set out in the following order: Yellow Ochre; Cadmium Yellow, light; Cadmium Yellow, medium; Cadmium Orange; Cadmium Red (extra scarlet); Selium Purple; Alizarin Crimson; Burnt Umber; and Burnt Sienna.

The cool colors are arranged as follows: Ultramarine Blue, deep; Cobalt Blue; Shiva Blue, deep; Payne's Grey; Shiva Green; Chrome Oxide Green, deep; Terra Verte; Ivory Black; and Titanium White.

For this painting I used Whatman board, rough. Gesso board, Masonite or any stiff board that is nonporous may be used for casein. The board need not be top quality inasmuch as the whole surface is covered with paint and the whiteness of the board itself does not become a part of the painting as it does in watercolor.

When using casein, brushes need special care. If the paint is allowed to dry on them, they will be ruined. After each painting session brushes must be washed thoroughly with a lanolin shampoo to keep them pliable.

"Deep Water" might be called a mood painting, a little on the illustrative side. The background—the turbulent sky and the windswept tree—sets the scene and plays the supporting role to the figure which dominates the picture. The story-telling quality in a painting is often dramatically heightened by the use of a figure.

The pose used in this painting is from a photograph I took of a small, introspective boy—about seven years old—sitting on top of a table. The picture was taken from a "worm's-eye-view"—looking up at the subject with my eye-level at the base of the figure. (This is the exact opposite of the "bird's-eye-view" described in painting "At the Beach" on page 40.) Both the size of the figure and its placement in the foreground, puts the emphasis on the face and its expression of pensive loneliness. One feels that the toy sailboat has lost its appeal to its owner and that even the approaching storm may not startle the boy out of his reverie.

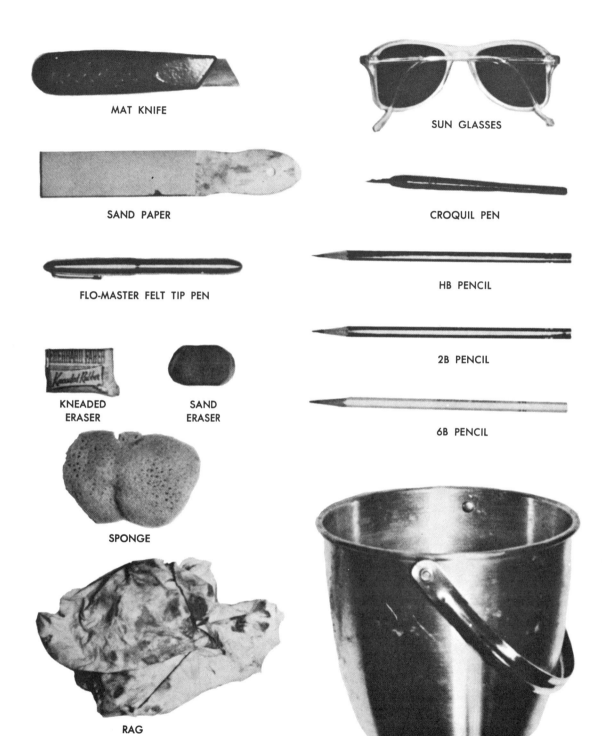

MAT KNIFE

SUN GLASSES

SAND PAPER

CROQUIL PEN

FLO-MASTER FELT TIP PEN

HB PENCIL

KNEADED
ERASER

SAND
ERASER

2B PENCIL

6B PENCIL

SPONGE

RAG

WATER BUCKET

V. MATERIALS

AND HOW TO USE THEM

It is extremely important for the serious artist to use top quality materials. He should learn from the start what good materials can do for him, rather than form painting habits with second-rate materials. No amount of acquired skill can compensate for fading colors or buckling paper; poor brushes only make a hard task harder. The saying, "A craftsman is no better than his tools" is more than just a cliché. As there are many reputable art supply houses that manufacture materials of good quality, the choice of brands is up to the artist—to determine by his own experimentation.

In line with this, the brand of colors used is a matter of the artist's preference. In my work I use Rembrandt colors but other brands are preferred by many artists. Whatever brand you use, be sure it is top grade for depth of color, permanency, easy application and manipulation.

Good quality paper is essential for watercolor painting. I prefer heavy, handmade rag papers because of their weight and irregular surface. The paintings reproduced in color in this book were painted on this type of paper —300-pound D'Arches, 400-pound American Watercolor Society, and 400-pound Royal Watercolor Society. Most commercial papers have a stamped pattern surface that gives the effect of a reproduction upon close inspection. They also buckle and wrinkle under heavy washes, and cannot be worked over to any degree without serious injury to the painting. However, they are useful when a smoother texture is desired. For the black and white illustrations in this book I used Strathmore, Crescent Board, and 200-pound Saunders paper.

Watercolor sable brushes in several sizes are shown in the photograph on page 114, along with other types of brushes I find useful. They will be discussed in detail on page 115 and the following pages.

In addition other equipment is needed by the watercolorist. Some essential accessories are shown on the facing page. They include a water bucket, paint rags, a mat knife, sandpaper, kneaded and sand erasers, HB, 2B, and 6B pencils, a Flo Master pen, and sun glasses. In painting out-of-doors, sun glasses eliminate the blinding glare of the white paper, and help the artist to see values more clearly. However, they must be of good quality or they will change the appearance of the colors on the palette.

THE PALETTE

The palette used for most of the paintings in this book is the same wide-range palette that I use for landscapes because in many instances the child is part of the scape.

However, for the paintings without backgrounds or with very simple backgrounds, I have used limited palettes of three to five colors.

I use a 13- by 19-inch white enamel butcher's tray for my palette and arrange the colors around the edge in perimeter fashion, the warm earth colors first, then the cold colors and last, the black. The center of the tray is left free for mixing.

It is helpful to keep the same palette arrangement at all times so that you can learn to know where each color is placed. You will soon be able to find the color you want automatically, thus saving time and mistakes.

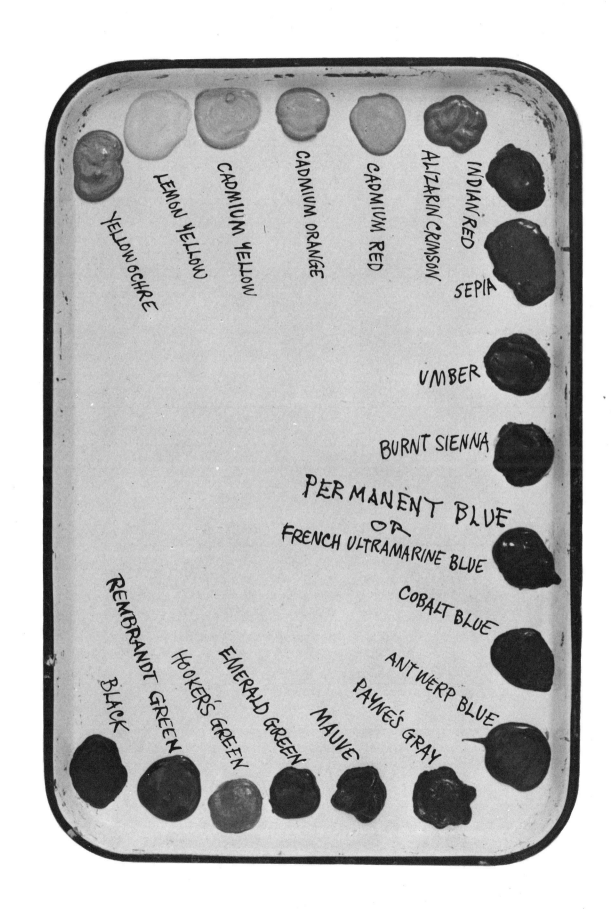

YELLOW OCHRE

LEMON YELLOW

CADMIUM YELLOW

CADMIUM ORANGE

CADMIUM RED

ALIZARIN CRIMSON

INDIAN RED

SEPIA

UMBER

BURNT SIENNA

PERMANENT BLUE
OR
FRENCH ULTRAMARINE BLUE

COBALT BLUE

ANTWERP BLUE

PAYNE'S GRAY

MAUVE

EMERALD GREEN

HOOKER'S GREEN

REMBRANDT GREEN

BLACK

MIXING PAINT

In the painting instructions in this book, I refer to mixing paint on the palette and mixing it on the paper. These terms may have raised questions in your mind about their exact meaning and why the distinction is so important. The two methods of applying color produce entirely different effects. This should be clearly understood so you will know why and under what circumstances to use each method.

The photographs shown above illustrate quite graphically what is meant by mixing on the palette—the usual way of mixing color.

Color that is mixed on the paper is applied onto the paper in separate daubs of pure color and then blended together. As an example, the photographs shown below demonstrate how

this method is used in painting dark hair. Small daubs of Permanent Blue, Burnt Sienna, Sepia, Black, and Antwerp Blue are applied to the paper in any sequence and blended together. The effect is a vibrant undercoating. Only a minimum of overpainting is necessary to give depth of color and form. If these five colors had been mixed on the palette before applying them, the resulting color would be a very deep, dull, grayed green, without any nuances.

The principal use of this method of mixing color is to produce an undercoating. Its purpose is to eliminate the flat opaque effect so common in many watercolors, both landscapes and portraits. However, it is sometimes used without any overpainting.

This method of applying color was used extensively in the paintings, "Portrait of a Girl and Her Doll" (frontispiece), "At the Beach" (page 41), and "Comaraderie" (page 111).

CAMARADERIE

With their arms around each other in a tender gesture of love and devotion, these two friends gaze in fascination at the sea, unconsciously assuming a pose of protector and protected. These two little girls, about three and five years old, were photographed at the seashore near my home town. As is no doubt evident, the water holds a fascination for me too. The pencil sketches on page 113 point up the fact that I first tried to place the figures against a simpler background, but after considerable thought, I felt that the water setting would give the picture more meaning and interest.

PAINTING INSTRUCTIONS FOR CAMARADERIE

Size of original painting—28 by 20 inches.
Paper—300-pound D'Arches.

Step 1.   Dampen the sky area with a not-too-wet sponge, and paint a thin wash of Yellow Ochre over the damp area, using a 2-inch brush. Add a wash of Permanent Blue at top of sky and water. While still damp, wipe out the faint cloud with a clean rag.

Step 2.   When the horizon is almost dry, cover water area with a light wash of Antwerp Blue and a touch of Sepia; use a 2-inch brush working in horizontal brush strokes. Wipe out the breaker in foreground with a clean sponge, again using horizontal strokes. Be careful to clean the sponge between each stroke so that the color will not be reapplied. For the wet sandy portion of foreground use Orange, Burnt Sienna and Permanent Blue, mixed on the paper.

Step 3.   Paint the flesh areas with a wash of Lemon Yellow and Burnt Sienna, mixed on palette, using a number 12 brush. While still damp add a touch of Mauve on the edges of the legs and arms. When dry, paint dark accents with Burnt Sienna and Mauve, mixed on palette, and model. Paint the dark hair with Black, Sepia, Burnt Sienna, and Permanent Blue, mixed on the paper. Put a wash of Lemon Yellow and Medium Yellow over the blonde hair. When dry, add Burnt Umber, Sepia, and Burnt Sienna for the darker areas, mixing the colors on the paper. Keep the edges soft, blending with a number 12 brush. For the shadows on the white dress, use Permanent Blue, Orange, and Indian Red, mixed on the paper. Add a touch of Alizarin Crimson on the lower left portion reflecting the pink dress. Cover the pink dress with a light wash of Alizarin Crimson and a touch of Cadmium Red. When dry, apply a wash of Permanent Blue and Alizarin Crimson for the darker areas. Mix colors on the palette.

Step 4.   Paint the reflections of the figures on the shoreline with Burnt Sienna, Permanent Blue, and Sepia, mixed on paper. Use an Aquarelle brush, working in cross-wise horizontal brush strokes. Soften edges with a 1/4-inch bristle brush.

BILLOW SKY

REVERSE
POSITION

TALL
WEEDS

ON A HILL

LOW HORIZON LINE

LIGHT

Pleasant sky
not too busy

sea gulls

water
calm

Busy
weed

weed
shadow

SAND

Use pencil roughs to test poses and settings.

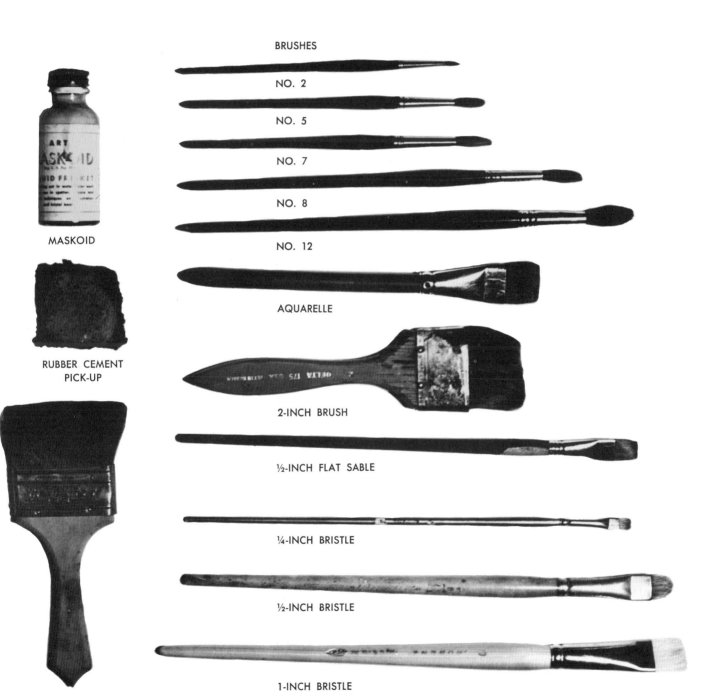

MASKOID

RUBBER CEMENT
PICK-UP

3-INCH BRUSH

BRUSHES

NO. 2

NO. 5

NO. 7

NO. 8

NO. 12

AQUARELLE

2-INCH BRUSH

½-INCH FLAT SABLE

¼-INCH BRISTLE

½-INCH BRISTLE

1-INCH BRISTLE

BRUSHES

Although much has been written about the necessity of using good quality brushes, this cannot be overemphasized. Much has also been written about applying color, brush strokes and effects, but very little about how brushes should be handled to achieve these effects.

To the practicing artist, it is no secret that much of the freedom or tightness in a painting results from the way in which he holds the brush. It is most important to remember that the brush must be held loosely—so loosely that it can be knocked out of the hand with only a slight tap. For detail work the brush is held a little tighter but never in a vise-like grip.

There are two general movements for using the brush, and for each movement the brush is held in a different basic position. An arm movement is used for all large areas, and in some paintings it is used exclusively throughout. The photograph at left below shows how to hold the brush for the arm movement. A wrist movement is used primarily for detail work. The photograph at right below shows the position for the wrist movement, which is similar to the way a pen is held for writing.

Most inexperienced painters are afraid to

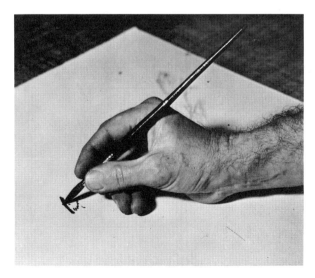

use large brushes, perhaps because of the mistaken idea that small brushes afford better control of the medium. No idea could be more suicidal. For very large areas I use an inexpensive, soft 3-inch brush as shown in the photograph at top left. A large brush such as this can be used for skies, large expanses of water, snow fields, houses, and so forth. It is a labor-saving device in that one stroke can do the work of many and the result is a fresher, looser painting. A 2-inch brush, pictured at middle left, is also useful.

The over-all size of the painting and the specific area involved will to a great extent determine the size brush to be used. In general, use the size brush that fits the scale of the area you are painting. However, a small brush need not necessarily be used for detail work. A large brush used in certain areas keeps the color flowing and prevents a patchy, overworked look. This is illustrated in the photograph at bottom right of the facing page. It is better to err on the side of using brushes that are too large rather than too small.

In my own work I use a considerable number of brushes but some painters think that it is unnecessary to be that extravagant. Of all the brushes available I would say that the Aquarelle is the most versatile and important. If I were limited to two brushes I would choose this and perhaps a number 8 sable watercolor brush.

The Aquarelle is 1-inch wide but its sable is much shorter than other 1-inch brushes (about ½-inch long), and comes to an edge like a chisel. It can be used flat for large areas while the fine edge can be used for details and to delete lights out of a dark background. In the photograph shown directly above, the heel of the Aquarelle is held flat against the paper so that the hairs of the brush barely touch the rough surface; it is dragged over the paper horizontally to give the effect of texture.

In the sable watercolor brushes, numbers 2, 5, 7 and 8 are used for detail work. In the large, sable watercolor brushes, either number 11 or 12 is ample. (A number 12 is pictured at right.) Such a brush is a costly luxury and should be treated with respect.

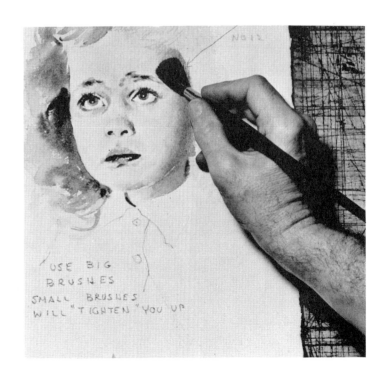

I also use ¼ and ½-inch short-hair flat sable oil brushes because, under certain circumstances, they make it easier to control the width of a stroke and give a more direct unworked-over look. The photograph at top left illustrates this use of a ½-inch flat sable oil brush. In addition I use short-hair bristle oil brushes to soften hard edges, as shown in the photograph directly below.

THE FAN BRUSH

The fan brush has long been familiar to the oil painter. Since its redesign with a shorter handle and a wider sable, it has become a valuable brush for the watercolorist. It is useful in producing a great variety of different effects. Not only does it reduce the number of strokes required to get the desired effect, but it gives a freer feeling.

Among its many uses is the painting of such things as weeds. This is done with an upward stroke starting at the base as shown in the photograph directly above. I use it also at times to paint leaves on trees, as shown in the photograph at upper right. This is done by patting the paint on with the heel of the brush. The result is a more delicate, indefinite shape than could be painted with a round brush, and gives the effect of many leaves without actually painting them.

Another use is in painting the grainy texture of wood. This is also done with an upward stroke, but with slightly more pressure applied. The brush is held closer to the heel and is dragged up with a slight waver to vary the grainy effect, as shown at left. However, this can be done only on smooth paper such as Strathmore which was used here. The completed painting is reproduced below on this page. These are some of the most helpful ways in which I use this brush, but I am sure that by experimenting you will find countless additional uses for it.

POSITION

OF THE PAPER

In general, a watercolor painting is executed with the paper in two alternating positions: upright and flat. The drawing is done with the paper in a relatively upright position; the preliminary and intermediate stages of painting, with the paper lying flat; and the final stages of painting, with the paper again upright.

There are good practical reasons for this. Unless the drawing is done with the paper upright, there will be distortion. On the other hand, unless the lay-in washes and intermediate wet stages are applied with the paper lying flat, the color will obviously run off the paper. However, since the final stages are painted much drier, it is expedient to work vertically again. This makes it possible to get farther away from the paper from time to time to see the picture as a whole—lessening the danger of patchy painting and ensuring a more unified picture.

THE SPONGE

A soft silk cosmetic sponge is valuable both as a tool and as an accessory brush. I use it for deleting lights in dark areas, and for washing out mistakes, as well as for special effects such as clouds, sky, water, fog, rain, and sea. The photographs shown here demonstrate its use in reducing the intensity of color. A coarse grained sponge can be used with a patting or dabbing motion for rougher textures such as gravel and stucco.

MASKOID

In painting a scene such as "In a Field of Daisies," the artist has one of three choices: using opaque white; painting around the white areas; or using Maskoid to preserve the whites.

As a purist watercolor painter, I do not approve of using opaque white. Unless it is used by a skilled craftsman the effect is muddy-looking and the painting loses the transparency and freshness of a pure watercolor.

The practice of painting around white areas is not only difficult, but usually results in a pasted-in look. For ease of execution and maintaining fluidity in a painting, I prefer to use Maskoid on the white areas, and to paint over the Maskoid. When it is removed, the white areas may be left white, or partly toned in accordance with the subject matter.

Maskoid is a thin liquid, masking solution that forms a waterproof film when it dries. More pliable and versatile than other types of rubber cement, it is applied with a brush in the same way as opaque white. Use an inexpensive brush, taking care to clean it thor-oughly after using in a rubber-cement solvent and thinner such as Bestine. Avoid using Maskoid in direct hot sun as it has a tendency to become gummy if exposed to heat. It should not be left on the paper for more than a month as it becomes impossible to remove after a longer period. Otherwise it is easily removed when dry with a rubber-cement pick-up or a piece of dried Maskoid.

VI. PORTFOLIO
OF CANDID PHOTOGRAPHS

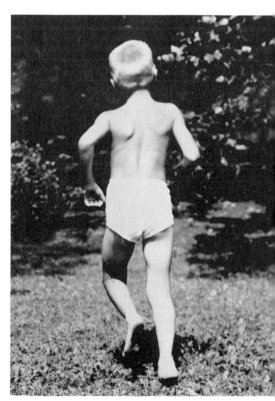

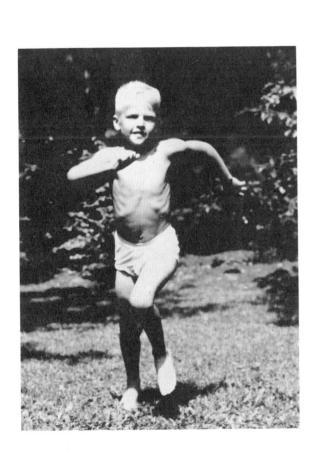

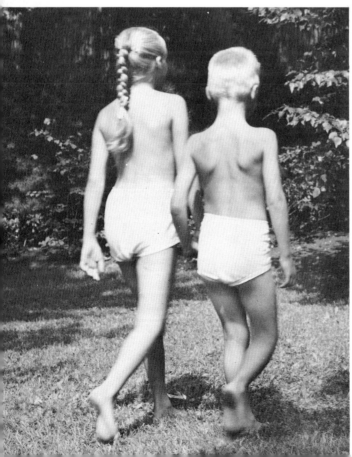

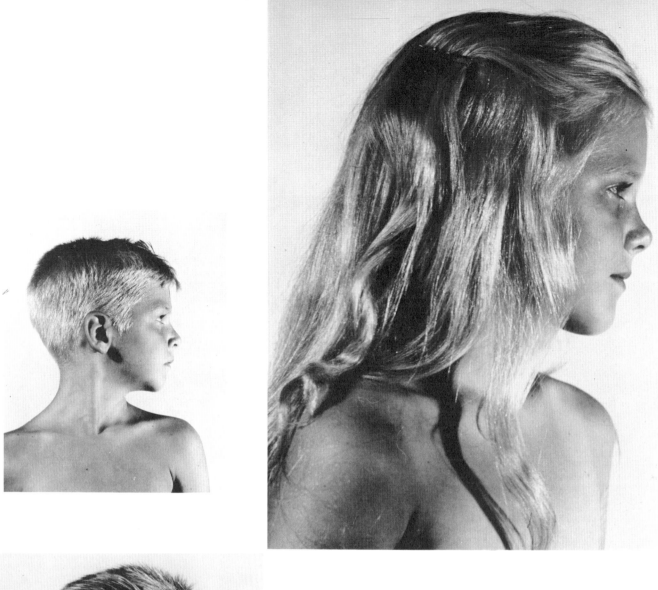

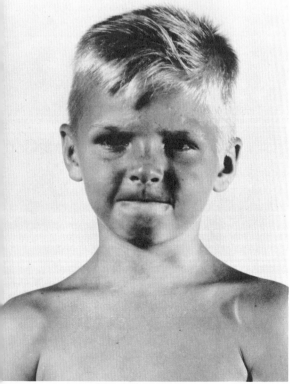

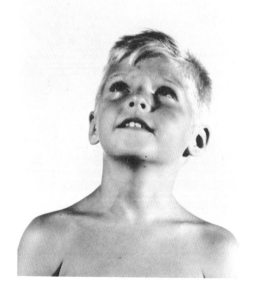